CW00432300

CONTENTS

2-7

THE IMPORTANCE
OF STORIES

8

THE KEY ELEMENTS
OF STORYTELLING

9-19

CHARACTER

20-25

CONFLICT

26-27

PLOT

28-35

BRAND STORYTELLING

THE IMPORTANCE OF STORIES THROUGH TIME

If you look it up in the dictionary, it will tell you that a story is "an account of imaginary or real people and events told for entertainment"; "a plot or storyline". Well, this is all well and true, but the importance of stories through time shouldn't be underestimated. The art of storytelling has seen cultures develop traditions and superstitions; religions all around the world gain millions of devoted followers through the stories they tell; and more recently, we have seen businesses become well-loved brands by appealing to our emotions.

Stories bring people, places, and events to life,
acting as fundamental learning tools that allow
us to reflect on the past and imagine a better future.

They are ubiquitous — we all 'get' stories,
no matter where we're from.

They are contagious — tell a story to someone,
and if it resonates it will spread; the most powerful
stories demand to be retold, again and again.

They stick — through the re-telling, they embed
themselves in our own and our shared memory.

WHY DO WE TELL STORIES?

According to Evolutionists, we have transferred knowledge and shared understanding through storytelling for generations. Tales, fables, whatever you want to call them, they're "sticky". They find a space and burrow in a corner of our minds, becoming a shared memory as we retell them.

Psychologists believe that our brains are hard-wired to tell stories and that we innately know how to construct them, whilst sociologists say that the telling of stories brings communities together.

And how or why do things change? They expose us to human truths and build a sense of community through a shared emotional understanding.

Great stories help us make sense of our lives and teach us valuable lessons, encouraging us to question **"what would happen if?"**

"The purpose of a storyteller is not to tell you how to think, but to give you questions to think upon."

– Brandon Sanderson, **The Way of Kings**

"Stories have to be told or they die, and when they die, we can't remember who we are or why we're here."

– Sue Monk Kidd, **The Secret Life of Bees**

"If a storyteller worried about the facts – my dear Lucian, how could he ever get at the truth?"

– Lloyd Alexander, **The Arkadians**

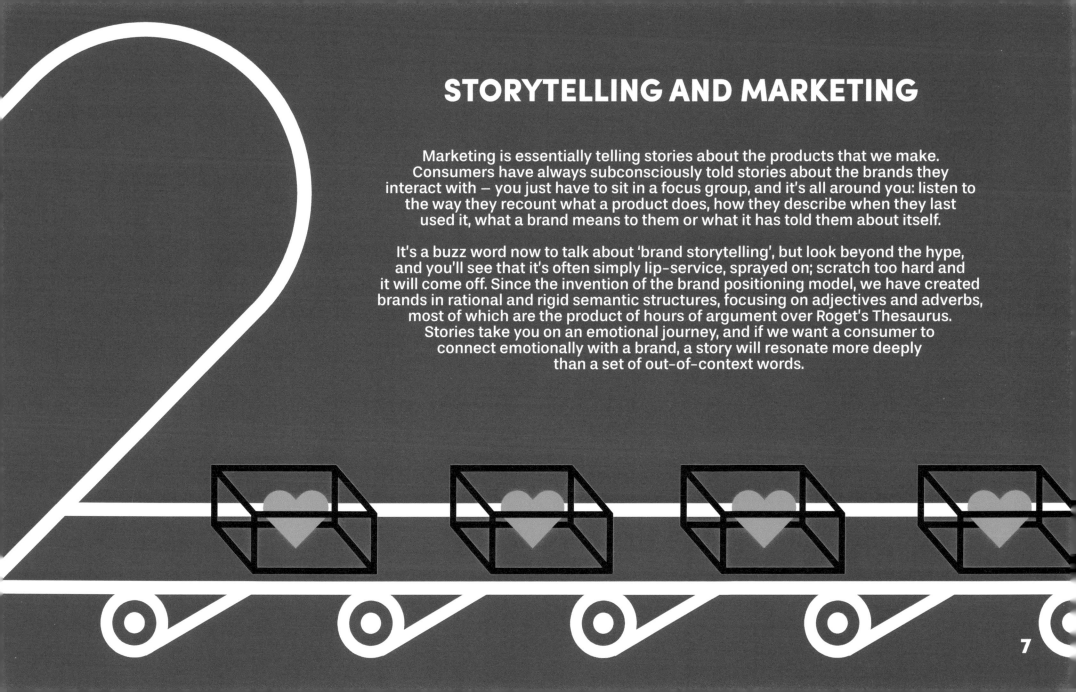

STORYTELLING AND MARKETING

Marketing is essentially telling stories about the products that we make. Consumers have always subconsciously told stories about the brands they interact with — you just have to sit in a focus group, and it's all around you: listen to the way they recount what a product does, how they describe when they last used it, what a brand means to them or what it has told them about itself.

It's a buzz word now to talk about 'brand storytelling', but look beyond the hype, and you'll see that it's often simply lip-service, sprayed on; scratch too hard and it will come off. Since the invention of the brand positioning model, we have created brands in rational and rigid semantic structures, focusing on adjectives and adverbs, most of which are the product of hours of argument over Roget's Thesaurus. Stories take you on an emotional journey, and if we want a consumer to connect emotionally with a brand, a story will resonate more deeply than a set of out-of-context words.

THE KEY ELEMENTS OF STORYTELLING

There are 3 elements to every story

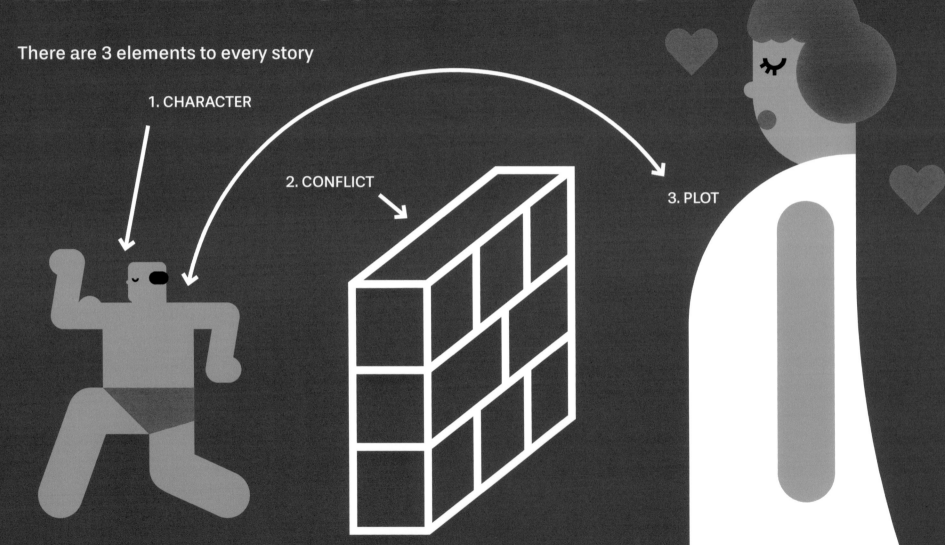

1. CHARACTER

2. CONFLICT

3. PLOT

1. CHARACTER

The best characters are ones that we take time to learn and understand: they are layered and complex, have strengths and weaknesses.

THE PROTAGONIST

A good story has a protagonist that really struggles.
The harder the situation is to overcome – the more the
protagonist needs to dig deep within himself, make difficult
decisions, take action despite risks – then the more
compelling the story.

Every protagonist has an 'immediate want', which is something that he
wants to achieve in the short term and is usually something functional.
During the course of the story, the emphasis shifts to his 'life need', as this
is his deeper motivation and what really drives him.

Every story needs a protagonist — the 'hero' of the story, though they don't have to act heroically.
And every protagonist needs a goal. The beginning of the story will establish a sense of normality
before identifying what it is that they need to achieve, before an inciting incident disrupts
the calm. The rest of the narrative is propelled by the choices that the protagonist makes
as they try to move towards their goal and restore a sense of balance.

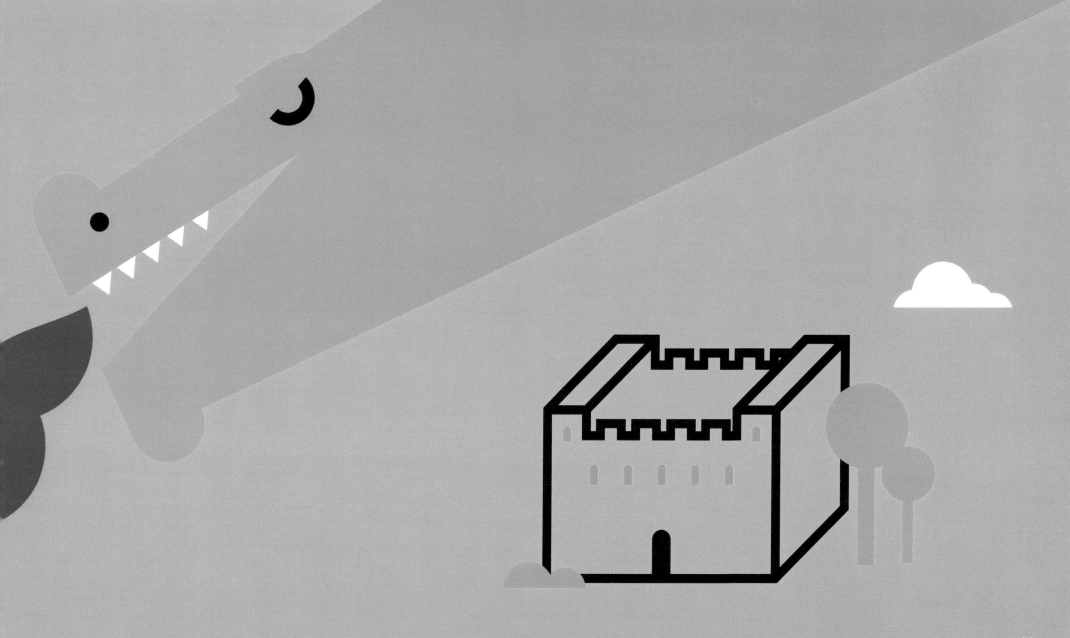

True character is revealed in the choices a human being makes under pressure – the greater the pressure, the deeper the revelation, the more we see the character's true essential nature.

Their character goes through a journey during the story, and this journey sees them end up somewhere different to where they started, learning lessons along the way. We begin to understand them and their complexities through the choices they make, and through these choices their fatal flaw is revealed – a weakness that they must eventually overcome.

All characters have to undergo change: they need to have a different perspective or attitude to how they were when they first started. Think about the Cary Grant character in It's a Wonderful Life: running through the streets with a new found joy about his life. This is the change that we love to see. There's usually a moment where things click into place for our protagonists, and they realise what they need to do to achieve their goal.

"Out of suffering have emerged the strongest souls; the most massive characters are seared with scars."

– Khalil Gibran

"Doubt is a question mark; faith is an exclamation point. The most compelling, believable, realistic stories have included them both."

– Criss Jami, **Killosophy**

JUNG'S ARCHETYPES

What makes a great protagonist is that we are all able to relate to him and understand him on a human level — no matter what culture or country you're from. Jung believed that there were personality types that we all innately understand and relate to; he defined these as 'Archetypes' that reside in the collective unconscious. So, whereas stereotypes (language we might use to describe the typical Banker or Builder) are culturally defined, Archetypes transcend culture, sharing fundamental values, strengths and weaknesses, and act as a common language.

EACH ARCHETYPE HAS:

Strengths that he will be able to use during the story

Vices or 'fatal flaws' present challenges and will need to be overcome in order to achieve his goals

THE 12 MASTER ARCHETYPES

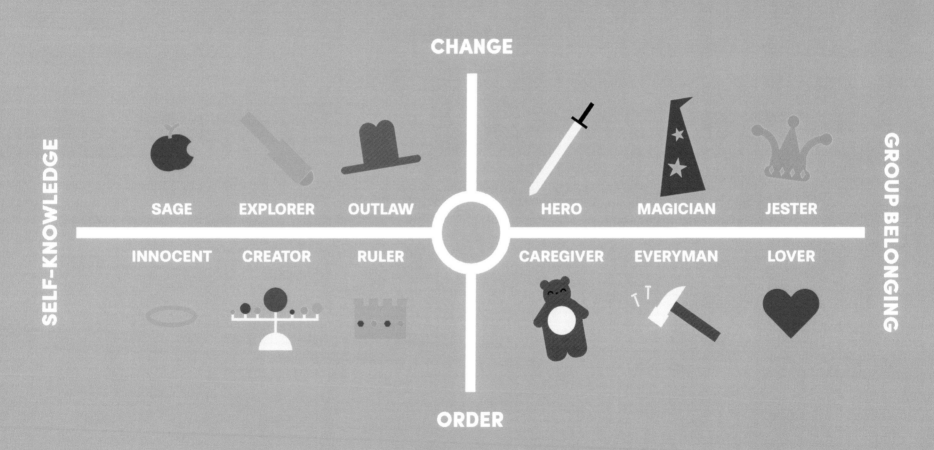

CHANGE

SELF-KNOWLEDGE

GROUP BELONGING

SAGE   EXPLORER   OUTLAW   HERO   MAGICIAN   JESTER

INNOCENT   CREATOR   RULER   CAREGIVER   EVERYMAN   LOVER

ORDER

WE CLEARLY CONSTRUCT 'PERSONALITIES' FOR BRANDS

We can make sure that brands resonate more deeply by aligning them to a strong archetype and ensuring that all communications, developments and strategic decisions fit this archetype. By exploring brand archetypes within categories we can see where each brand sits in relation to each other, identifying spaces for differentiation. Though this is rarely discussed, the awareness of a brand's 'fatal flaws' would open up a conversation about what needs to happen in order for these to be overcome, leading to a stronger (and more realistic) storyline.

2. CONFLICT

"At their most basic, stories are about conflict and resolution – the basic tenets of life: man suffers difficulty and gets through it; we can all relate to this. We are attracted to the human strength to overcome."

— Rob Mckee

CONFLICT AND RESOLUTION ARE AT THE HEART OF EVERY STORY

It is the backbone of every story. Hollywood movie guru, Rob McKee, insists that there are 3 acts to every story:

A DISRUPTION OF THE STATUS QUO / AN ISSUE TO SORT

A STRUGGLE / CONFLICT

RESOLUTION / RETURN TO NORMALITY

WITHOUT CONFLICT, A STORY IS JUST DULL

There is no urgency, nothing to make us sit at the edge of our seats, no momentum. We see the most change in our hero when he is challenged most. Whether internal or external, the conflict is a disruption that sees our character struggle through dark moments before reaching a resolution that teaches them an important lesson.

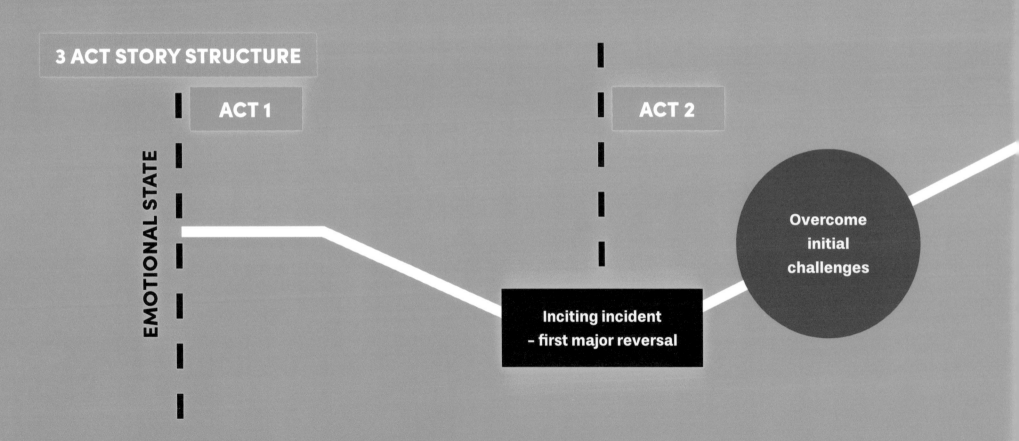

3 ACT STORY STRUCTURE

ACT 1

ACT 2

EMOTIONAL STATE

Inciting incident – first major reversal

Overcome initial challenges

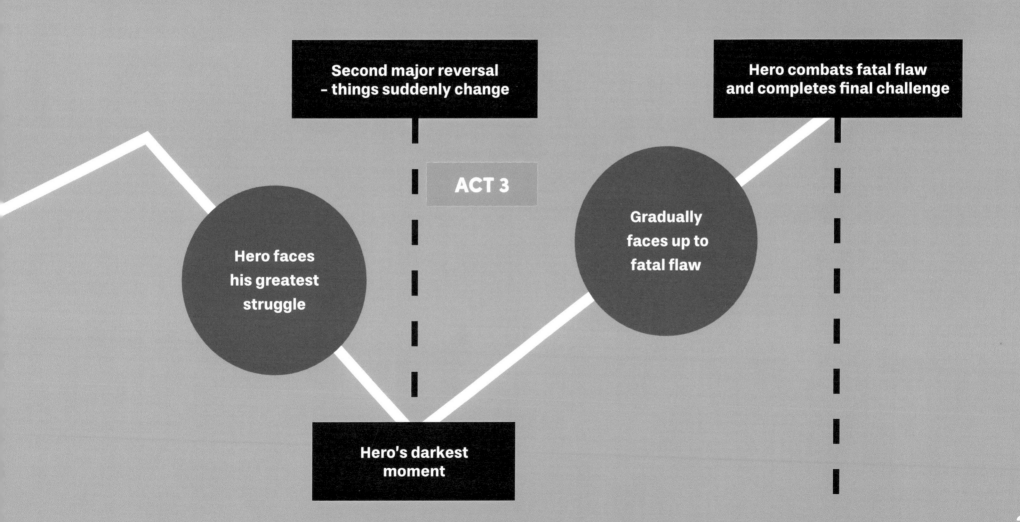

Second major reversal – things suddenly change

Hero combats fatal flaw and completes final challenge

ACT 3

Hero faces his greatest struggle

Gradually faces up to fatal flaw

Hero's darkest moment

IF YOU CAN CONNECT WITH PEOPLE ON AN EMOTIONAL LEVEL, YOU CAN TELL A MUCH STRONGER STORY

Essentially, we are emotional, limbic beings; it is very true that the things that succeed in this world, be they ideas or philosophies or people or, now, brands, are those which best connect with our emotions. 80% of decisions are made emotionally, not rationally. So, in this day and age where we are faced with infinite versions of the same product on a shelf, emotion is what counts.

"The best and most beautiful things in the world cannot be seen or even touched. They must be felt with the heart."

– Helen Keller

"But feelings can't be ignored, no matter how unjust or ungrateful they seem."

– Anne Frank, The Diary of a Young Girl

3. PLOT

"How small a quantity of real fiction there is in the world; and that the same images, with little variation, have served all the authors who have ever written."

— Dr. Samuel Johnson

THE PLOT HOLDS ALL OF THE STORY'S ELEMENTS AS A SUCCESSION OF ACTIONS AND REACTIONS

Influenced by Joseph Campbell, Christopher Booker studied many, many stories and identified 7 different plot types. Each plot type represents a different human value and teaches us the consequences of decisions.

1. Overcoming the Monster

To succeed, you will need to fight someone more powerful than you.

Strength, Stamina, Bravery

2. The Quest

Sometimes you have to put yourself in danger to make or find something of value.

Endurance, Determination

3. Voyage & Return

Don't be lured by false promises – appreciate what you've got now.

Wisdom, Curiosity

4. Rebirth

If you lose everything, it isn't always the end – everyone deserves a second chance.

Zeal, Optimism

5. Rags to Riches

Be true to yourself, and you will be rewarded.

Integrity, Purity

6. Tragedy

The punishment will suit the crime.

Humility, Tenacity

7. Comedy

Even complicated situations work out in the end.

Friendship, Love

BRAND EVOLVING THROUGH STORYTELLING

A story's sense of progression can be seen
implicitly in brands — they help us attain something
better than we had before. The message or promise
at the heart of the brand needs to echo this. Johnnie
Walker is a classic example of this: personal progress,
drive & ambition are key to this brand, and the striding
man symbolises this. Compare Johnnie Walker, about
progress, to Chivas, which reflects the status that you
have already attained. The latter is fundamentally static.
Imagine a film or a novel, where the hero has already
achieved what he needed to do — where can the story
go from there? He has nothing to do, to show, to
experience. So, all brands need to have an inherent
sense of progress innate to them — they have to
help move us from one state to another, but
they also have to evolve in themselves.

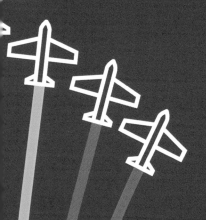

IDENTIFYING A BRAND'S PLOT TYPE

If there are only seven different storylines and every story we've ever told is simply a version of one of them, then perhaps we can say that there are only seven ways that a brand can grow and develop; a brand has to identify which plot is the most relevant for them and for their category. Is there a monster in the category that they need to overcome? Are they the Cinderella in their category? Are they on a quest to find something or do something out of the ordinary (Honda is perhaps one of the stronger examples of this story).

Once you've identified your story, you can drill down further into the dynamics of each plotline: the cast of other characters that assist the progression of the plot (both the goodies and the baddies), such as the Mentor, the Shapeshifter, as Christopher Vogler describes in his book, The Writer's Journey. All these characters can be mapped against your competitive and commercial landscape.

BRANDS CAN BE GREAT STORYTELLERS

Brands are like people — they have a name, personality, character and way of doing things; they have a point of view and build a reputation. With a clear understanding of how impactful stories can be, products and propositions can become living, breathing things that people love, remember and want to buy in to.

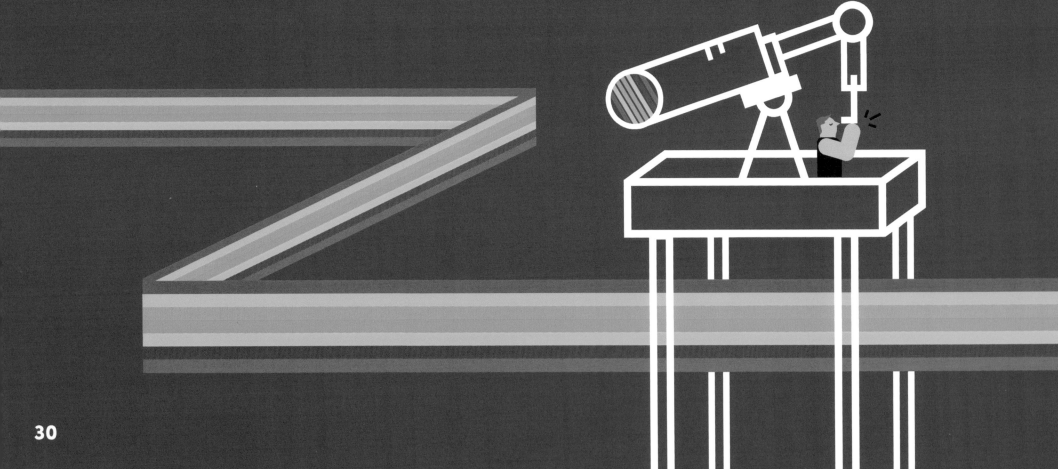

TELLING YOUR BRAND'S STORY

Each brand has been born to solve a problem, and this is the beginning of its story. So why does it exist, and how did it come to be? Growing through points of conflict, a brand's past has made it what it is today, and telling this story makes sense of why it speaks and behaves the way it does, untangling its complexities. A brand story helps make a commercial business feel human, and suddenly we as consumers are getting to know it a bit better.

DECLARING YOUR BRAND'S VISION

When we talk about the power of emotions, a brand's vision has the ability to inspire people — both those working within the company and those on the outside looking to buy in. What's the plot and what kind of world does it want to help create? Whether the brand is on a quest to change the status quo, or empower consumers so that they may overcome their inner monster, each brand vision should be an aspirational ambition that helps attract like-minded people.

TRANSPORTING CONSUMERS TO A DIFFERENT WORLD

Imagine if your brand could be a moment of escape for consumers — a window into a new world allowing them to escape the familiarity of their everyday. With the consumer as the hero of the brand's story, the product or service it is selling may act as a prop on a stage that has been set to give consumers an experience. Some of the most powerful and influential brands provide the tools for consumers to write their own story.

SO WHAT STORIES DOES YOUR BRAND
WANT TO TELL, AND HOW DO YOU
ENSURE THAT EACH IS AS ENGAGING
AND COMPELLING AS POSSIBLE?

We are **Butterfly London,** and we love to help brands tell their stories — whether launching new products, establishing a brand vision, or gathering insights to understand potential sources of conflict. Using a range of tools, we harness the power of storytelling to help brands cultivate a more meaningful, more human relationship with people.

We have a suite of tools that tap into the power of storytelling to help us build more powerful brands:

FAIRY TALE

Fairytale – Giving your brand a story to tell

Connecting with consumers on a more emotional, more meaningful level is hard
for brands. The power comes when we are able to cultivate a relationship
that was more natural, more human.

At Butterfly we appreciate that stories are a fundamental way in which human beings
make sense of the world at a deep unconscious level. We hear stories as children, we read
and watch stories as adults and we dream stories all through our lives. Telling stories
is how we bond and connect with one another.

Fairytale workshops harness the power of storytelling to give you resonating
brand positionings, communications platforms and product innovation.
Storytelling helps us build more powerful brands.

IDEALISER

Idealiser — Hitting the consumer hotspot with concept stories

You've got the core of an idea for a new product, but what will really make it hit the spot with your target consumer?

At Butterfly, we know how powerful stories can be in getting consumers involved and showing you how to make an idea fly. We ask consumers to join a quest to help the hero of our story (who just happens to be someone a lot like them) define their ideal product.

Idealiser allows them to pinpoint the features, benefits and reasons to believe they think are most compelling and create the tone of voice and visual style. You set the scene and start the plot; they tell you how to give your new product story a happy ending.

SAY HELLO

bianca@butterflylondon.com
M + 44 (0)7866 806 367 (UK)

DESIGNED BY

Ryan Dethy
ryan@butterflylondon.com